The Red Carpet

Guide *to* Visibility *and* Influence

Joie Gharrity

The Red Carpet Guide To Visibility and Influence

Copyright © 2016 by Joie Gharrity

ISBN-10: 0-692-69452-8
ISBN-13: 978-0-692-69452-7

For information regarding permission, write to:
The Zebra Ink
publisher@thezebraink.com

Printed in the United States of America

Copyeditor: Angela Mosley
Cover Design: Heather Robison
Interior Formatting: OneVoiceCan.com

The Zebra Ink, 3896 Dewey Avenue #196, Rochester, NY 14616
www.thezebraink.com

Order additional copies of this book today on
Amazon.com

Dear Mama G,

I want to thank you for your support and encouragement to always follow my dreams and to never define myself by other people's standards throughout the years. You have always praised my strengths while offering me the encouragement I needed to overcome adversity. It is because of you that I have found the strength and courage to swing for the stars. I am so very proud to be your daughter.

TABLE OF CONTENTS

THE TRAILER

I wanted to make a change in my life.

I wasn't sure what or how, but I knew the first step was to return to my hometown after spending a majority of my adult life living in Los Angeles and working in the Hollywood entertainment industry.

I was feeling uneasy about the move. I didn't truly have a sense of self. I dove into self-development in hopes that I would discover who I was and how I wanted to show up in the world.

The first major revelation came on a vacation on the cliffs of Maui. I had been suffering for more than thirteen years over the death of my brother. I jumped into self-development to find peace and freedom. A spiritual advisor had recommended that while I was in Maui I try a powerful healing ritual that could benefit me.

The ceremony seemed relatively simple. It involved a letter, a beautiful bottle, some Maui sand, and the "perfect" place to throw the bottle into the ocean. I was assured that this simple but symbolic ceremony would greatly help me heal and energetically help my family heal as well.

I kept thinking about finding the perfect bottle, writing the perfect letter, and finding the most amazing spot on the island for the ritual.

I imagined that I would purchase the most beautiful adorned bottle covered with jewels, glitter, and flowers. I combed the resort gift shops looking for the bottle. It didn't occur to me that at a five star resort, the Grand Wailea, this would be a tall order. On the last day of my trip I had no choice but to purchase a cheap bottle of wine and borrow an oversized black permanent marker from the front desk to decorate the bottle.

I imagined myself sitting on the beach and writing an eloquent letter to my brother that poetically described all the pain and loss that I had felt over the years.

Instead the only sentence that I was able to write over and over again was "I miss you."

I imagined myself under a large and beautiful waterfall where I would whisper a few words and place the bottle under the falls to rest for eternity.

The closest waterfall was on the other side of the island; I did not have transportation, and I was running out of time. I decided to take my message in the bottle to the highest point on the scenic trail overlooking the ocean a couple miles away from the resort.

I packed the bottle to the rim with Maui sand that made the bottle very heavy. I walked and walked on the twisted scenic trail looking for the perfect spot so that I could be alone. I finally decided on this one particular spot because, quite frankly, it was hot. The edge of the cliff was about fifteen feet away from the trail. The cliff was fenced in with wire so we tourists wouldn't go down with our bottles.

Doubt started creeping in about whether the bottle was going to clear the cliff and actually hit the water. After all I was a dancer as a child and never cared to play baseball or football. I told myself to believe and go for it!

I said a few words honoring my brother and my family. I took one last look around to make sure I was alone and with all my might I threw the bottle. I watched it soar over the cliff and my heart leaped with joy. I was so proud of myself.

As I eagerly listened for the splash ten stories below…

I heard an abrupt plunk and my heart skipped a beat. At that exact moment a beautiful woman jogging by with her Chihuahua stopped and said, "I don't think it made it" and her Chihuahua looked up at me shaking his head. I was mortified.

As I watched the duo jog away I heard my internal critics scream:

"You failed. If you can't do something right then don't bother doing it at all. That wasn't perfect, that was the farthest thing from perfect. Why did you insist on taking dance lessons? If you had only played catch with your dad like he wanted. You have let everyone down. Now Gavin will never cross over."

THE RED CARPET GUIDE TO VISIBILITY AND INFLUENCE

And then I stopped. "First of all, Gavin passed over 13+ years ago. I loved dance class, and frankly sports didn't interest me. I don't think my dad ever asked me to play catch." I laughed so hard I cried.

It occurred to me that my "internal critics" had been hogging my spotlight, keeping me from being visible and keeping me in the shadows. If I wasn't going to be my biggest cheerleader, then how could I expect others to honor and love me? The only way I was going to be able to be free of the pain and suffering was to forgive myself first. Then I needed to allow myself to be visible and stand strong in my spotlight.

At that moment I forgave myself, and I gently spoke to my "internal critics" and asked them to leave. Stepping back into my spotlight felt amazing.

As I began walking down the path back towards the resort, a beautiful butterfly flew right up to me, and I gazed upon its beauty. I heard my brother's laugh as if he were standing right next to me. We laughed together as I continued down the path. He escorted me all the way back to my room.

That day, I set an intention that I would launch a business. I was going to stand in my spotlight and be my own brand. Finally I felt that I knew who I was and how I wanted to show up – powerful. Standing in my spotlight and shining bright because it is my birthright.

As I was launching my company, 113 Branding, I had another big aha moment.

I realized that there is a big difference between being "in" service and being "of" service. When I worked in the studio systems, which are just large corporations, I was *in* service. When you work for powerful and well-known companies, you are handed millions of dollars of influence with built-in systems. There is not very much freedom to be *of* service to anyone outside of the corporation. That doesn't offer as much security as you would think. Often there is the added fear that at any time the influence and the security can all be taken away.

When I returned to my hometown and decided that I was going to be an entrepreneur, I had to start from scratch because I literally had no influence nor did I have my own personal or professional brand. I saw that the in service business model makes us dependent.

I declared that I would only be of service moving forward. I would no longer be dependent but rather build my own influence, personal and professional brands, and be of service to other entrepreneurs globally to help them do the same.

Being an entrepreneur has been one of the greatest challenges of my life. I had to decompress from an in service model, and it took a few years. During the process, I had yet another aha moment and this is that our influence is directly linked to our brand's earning power. In order to gain more influence as an entrepreneur, you have to get visible in the marketplace.

I created a branding system that I refer to as Song & Verses. I help entrepreneurs identify the signal they want to put out in the marketplace. That Song is supported by three verses and this is how we allow people to hook into us so we can get visible and grow the influence.

Discovering my song, which is the Visibility and Influence song, brought up a ton of feelings for me because what I realized is that when the song is in alignment, it is actually one of our key life lessons. It made so much sense that I loved working in the Hollywood entertainment industry and helping others get visible and grow their influence. I took a back seat because I was running away from my life lesson.

Don't misunderstand me. I loved working in the entertainment business. It was an incredible life changing experience where I learned valuable skills and strategies in business, branding, marketing, and more. When I put my "song" into action and my Visibility and Influence started growing, it was incredibly uncomfortable for me initially. Standing in my life lesson has allowed me to grow and stretch as a person and shine brightly.

Today, I have real purpose and because I am in alignment and singing my song, my brand is soaring higher and higher.

I encourage you to incorporate the exercises, strategies, techniques, and tips enclosed. Become visible and grow your influence. It is your birthright to shine bright and stand in your spotlight.

You are loved and appreciated!

Cheers,

Joie Gharrity

You are the Brand.
Everything else is just an
accessory.

113 BRANDING

VIP TICKET:
YOU ARE THE BRAND

You Are The Brand
Everything Else Is Just An Accessory

A brand is more than your business name or logo used to represent your business, services, and products.

It is the emotional connection that a person makes with your business, services, and products based on the signals you are putting out in the marketplace.

In other words you are the brand and everything else is just an accessory.

We all have a spotlight that we are standing in. The bigger the Visibility and Influence spotlight you build for your brand the more you will open yourself up to success, fans, wealth, opportunities, fame, criticism...

Your inner game plays a major part in breaking through roadblocks so that your brand can soar higher and higher. It is worth the time and effort to make sure your inner game is on track. Paying attention to my inner game is what has led to my success as a brand.

Let's explore your inner game so you have a solid foundation to build your influence on.

~EXERCISE~
Your Inner Critics

Every person has internal critics that can stop them from making progress with their Visibility and Influence. I had to identify some of my Inner Critics, and I used this exercise to keep them in the shadows so that I could shine brightly which is my birthright.

Put a check mark next to your Inner Critics:

_____ "Little Miss Perfect"
Do you try to be perfect in every way so as not to be criticized?

_____ "Mr. Fear"
Is fear in the driver's seat? Are your decisions made from a fearful place?

_____"Mrs. Procrastination"
Do you put things off rather than make a mistake or be criticized?
Are your decisions pushed off or ignored completely?

_____"Mr. I Am Not Smart Enough"
Do you believe people will think that you are not smart enough or
that you have not acquired enough education?

_____"Ms. Who Cares About My Story"
Do you believe that your story does not matter or that you do not
have any relevant stories to share?

_____"Mr. I Am Too Old"
Do you believe there is a timeline on your talents and that your age
plays a factor on moving forward?

_____"Ms. I Am Not Skinny Enough"
Do you believe that until you look a certain way and weigh a
certain amount you can't go for your dreams?

Make a list of your own Inner Critics:

Next, say hello to your Inner Critics' Corner. Imagine them all sitting around a table and chatting. Pretend to be a fly on the wall and listen very carefully to your Inner Critics. As you listen write down what you hear. (It can be full blown sentences or perhaps just key words.)

Now imagine yourself walking your Inner Critics out the front door and slamming the door shut. Now you have permission to say, "THE END!"

Your Inner Critics have been hogging your spotlight and they no longer serve you. Instead, it is about celebrating you and your journey. When you are your biggest cheerleader, the world will support your brand, product, and services.

Write "The End!" ten times and imagine walking your Inner Critics out the front door.

~EXERCISE~
EXTERNAL CRITICS

In Hollywood we have a saying, "Everyone Is A Critic."

Now that we have worked on the Inner Critics let's talk External Critics. You know the ones - family, friends, co-workers, significant others...

The long and short of it is, no matter what you do or how well you do it, there will always be someone who doesn't get or like your brand, product, and services. It is a fact. There is nothing you can do about it.

The key is forgiveness.

Repeat the following when you are feeling criticized by others. *"I forgive those who do not support me. I send them love. It is my birthright to shine bright. I love myself and it is a gift to share my talents with the world."*

~EXERCISE~
WRITE YOURSELF A FAN LETTER

Sometimes you need to remind yourself of why you deserve the spotlight. You have been given talents and gifts that you are sharing with others. There is nothing wrong with recognizing the things that you have been given and that you use in being of service to others.

Rave about all the wonderful things you've been doing. Gush about you and how amazing you are.

Write yourself a fan letter.

Place the letter in an envelope, address it to yourself and add postage. Give it to a trusted friend and ask that they mail it to you the following year. You will be delighted to hear from yourself and to remind yourself how special and spectacular you really are.

PROPS FOR SHINING IN YOUR SPOTLIGHT

1. MEDITATION CAN BRING YOUR GOALS INTO SHARPER FOCUS

Did you know that you can harness your drive through meditation and attract even better opportunities into your professional life? Perhaps you might have heard about the benefits of meditation, yet you could never imagine spending hours focusing on your navel when you have deadlines to meet and products to launch. Meditation has come a long way since the days of monks sitting cross-legged on a mountaintop. Now, you can allow your light to shine even brighter by utilizing these three simple steps to meditation that will ease your stress while bringing your goals into sharper focus.

Meditate Daily

113 BRANDING

✦ Define Your Intention

Although meditation in itself is a great stress-reliever, to get what you want, you will need to define your intention. To do so, simply brainstorm a few of the things you would like to achieve. No achievement is too large to include on this list, so go ahead and dream big. Then, create a positive statement that can be used as your mantra. Once you have defined your intentions, you can focus on one or two each day or go through the entire list as if it were a script.

✦ Meditate Every Day

For meditation to be effective, it should be done every day. While a good meditation session should last about 20-minutes, it is also possible to include short meditation sessions throughout your day. As you meditate, relax your mind and clear out all of your distractions. Remember, this time is about focusing your energy on fulfilling your goals. If a stray thought enters your mind, acknowledge it and return to your defined intentions. Over time, it will become easier to let your mind relax and focus solely on your meditations.

✦ Visualize to Make It Real

The key to successful meditation is visualization. As you breathe in and out slowly, be sure to feel the emotions that come with obtaining all that you desire. Remember to focus on the understanding that your dreams are within your grasp. Each one will be fully realized as you rely on the fundamental truth that everything you need is already within the Universe, just waiting to be brought out by the adventuresome spirit that makes you unique.

2. Brag! The Art Of Tooting Your Own Horn

We have been taught that it is not polite to "brag." But how are people going to support you if they have no idea who you are or what you do? A great way to emotionally connect with the marketplace is through storytelling.

You want to be authentic. When you are authentically speaking from your heart and sharing your personal and professional stories in the marketplace, it allows people to emotionally connect with your brand, products, and services. Your stories matter and standing in your spotlight and shining bright is your birthright.

~EXERCISE~

WRITE A FEW LINES THAT DESCRIBE A STORY YOU CAN SHARE IMMEDIATELY WITH THE MARKETPLACE.

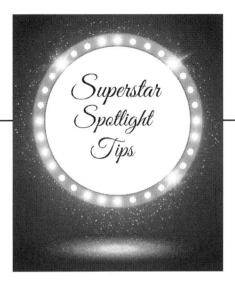

Superstar Spotlight Tips

1. Respect the time and generosity of those who help and support you. Send them a branded thank you note, as it can go a long way in showing your gratitude.

2. Be early to every meeting, as it will reflect nicely on your brand.

3. Always follow through. Nothing builds a business relationship faster than being a reliable brand.

4. While at a networking event, give your complete attention to the person you are speaking with.

5. Create branded products that you can sell online.

~EXERCISE~
FILL IN FIVE OF YOUR OWN TIPS THAT YOU CAN SHARE WITH THE MARKETPLACE.

Your
Brand
Visibility
and
Influence is
directly linked
to your
earning
power.

113 BRANDING

ACT I:

Your Brand in the Spotlight

$\mathcal{G}$ain greater Visibility and Influence by clearly telling your customer what they can expect when they interact with your company brand. Aligning your company-branded "song," or in other words "your signal," leverages your emotional connection with your customer. It is key to calling in your Ideal Client.

~EXERCISE~

CREATE A LIST OF QUALITIES THAT
DESCRIBE YOUR IDEAL CLIENT

TAKE 1: TESTIMONIALS

Incorporate testimonials that represent your Ideal Client, both written and video, into your company brand.

This tells the marketplace who you work with and allows your Ideal Client to emotionally connect with you and your company brand.

Share them across your social media channels, on your website, and in your company brand marketing materials to gain greater Visibility and Influence in the marketplace.

For Example:

"Joie's expertise and content creation that stayed true to my brand and my message went well beyond my expectations."

Sheila Kennedy

~EXERCISE~
LIST THREE TESTIMONIALS THAT REPRESENT YOUR IDEAL CLIENT.

TAKE 2: IMAGERY

Incorporate imagery of you and your Ideal Client into your company brand.

This tells the marketplace who you work with and allows your Ideal Client to see themselves in the company brand.

Display these images on your company website and across your social media channels.

For Example:

JEN DUCHENE AND JOIE GHARRITY

~EXERCISE~
Reference three images that incorporate your Ideal Client.

TAKE 3: Intake Form

Incorporate an intake form into your company brand.

An intake form can help you identify your Ideal Client quickly and easily.

It can weed out potential clients who are not a good fit for you and your company brand. It is no secret that one bad experience with a client can literally close your company brand doors.

For example:

Questionnaire

Please answer all questions as thoroughly as possible. If you do not know the answer, please leave the space blank.

General Information

Name:
Company Name:
Who is your primary customer?
What are your most pressing problems or concerns right now with your business?
If you could create the perfect business, with no limits on what is possible, what would that business look like?

~EXERCISE~
LIST THREE QUESTIONS THAT WILL
HELP YOU IDENTIFY YOUR IDEAL CLIENT.

Your Brand Visibility and Influence Is Directly Linked To Your Earning Power

Entrepreneurs know that it can be very easy to get caught up in the workings of the business--creating content, systems, programs, and all those other things that need to be attended to daily. It is time-consuming, and working on the company brand's Visibility and Influence in the marketplace can take a backseat.

It is crucial that the process of creating your brand content integrates seamlessly with maximizing your Visibility and Influence in the marketplace. In other words, you want to be growing your company brand Visibility and Influence immediately because it is directly linked to your company brand's earning power.

Many entrepreneurs wait until everything is "perfect" before putting their brand out there in the marketplace. It is natural for people to want to make sure that anything people will see attributed to their name is in ideal order first. There are many reasons for this, but the following two are generally the most prevalent.

1. Fear of Criticism

The first is fear of being criticized. Socially, many entrepreneurs are told that everything needs to be "perfect," and if everything is not "perfect," then they will be criticized publicly and privately. It is important in business to personally separate yourself from your company because it takes time to grow the brand's Visibility and Influence, which is directly linked to increasing your customer base. Live your brand, day in and day out, and the customers will follow.

2. Lack of Confidence

The second is the lack of confidence. You are worthy of stepping out of the shadows and into the spotlight allowing the marketplace to see you and your company brand. You will feel uncomfortable at times, but your brand's earning power relies on you allowing the marketplace to see you and your company brand shining bright.

If you want your brand to be a six-figure business, your brand's Visibility and Influence in the marketplace needs to be at a six-figure level. Your brand's earning power is directly linked to your brand's Visibility and Influence. In order for customers to want to buy your products and services, they have to be able to easily find and trust your business.

Superstar Spotlight Tips

1. Share your company brand's unique point-of-view across your social media channels to gain greater Visibility and Influence in the marketplace.

2. It's not good enough to just have a website. Your website reflects your brand, so make it shine bright.

3. Maintain a low overhead and manage your cash flow effectively so that your brand has a chance to thrive.

4. Experts are not good at everything. They're amazing in their brand field.

5. Don't be afraid to give your branded content away for free. It is a way of building your reputation as an "expert."

EXERCISE:
FILL IN FIVE OF YOUR OWN TIPS THAT YOU CAN SHARE WITH THE MARKETPLACE.

Branding is like denim. It fits and feels better the more you wear it.
113 BRANDING

ACT II:
LEVERAGING YOUR BRAND INFLUENCE

*G*ain greater Visibility and Influence by being consistent in communications. In other words, a clear company brand marketing campaign tells your customers what they can count on from your products and services.

A marketing campaign should have multi-layers. It should include a topic or theme and then content to support the topic. The easiest way for an entrepreneur to accomplish this would be to choose a weekly theme. Layer in images, blog posts, videos and networking. Record what you are sharing weekly in your calendar. Make note of where you have posted each item, so you can review the analytics and track its success.

~EXERCISE~
"CREATE A FOUR WEEK MARKETING CALENDAR THAT YOU CAN EASILY REFER TO DAILY"

Week #1

Week #2

Week #3

Week #4

Take 1: Electronic Signature

Increase your consistency in communication by leveraging your electronic signature. Always display your company brand title.

Display your contact information along with all of your company brand's social media hyperlinks.

Include current professional content such as blog posts, articles, etc.

For Example:

113 BRANDING
Brand Strategist I Marketer I Speaker

M: 415.735.5613
W: 113branding.com
E: jg7light@gmail.com

LinkedIn I Facebook I Twitter I Pinterest I Google+

~EXERCISE~
Record all of your
significant information below:

TAKE 2: ARTICLE CONTENT

Increase your consistency in communications and of experience by building article content into your company brand.

Establish your "expertise" in every article by including actual tangible tools and techniques the marketplace can incorporate easily.

Incorporate your company brand's unique point-of-view into your article content building so that the marketplace can emotionally connect with you and your company brand.

FOR EXAMPLE: 113 BRANDING VIRTUAL MAGAZINE ARTICLE SPOTLIGHT STARRING LISA LAMONT, LIFE AND BUSINESS INTUITIVE ADVISOR, HYPNOTHERAPIST, AUTHOR AND SPEAKER

"My one-of-a-kind Gypsy Cards along with my intuitive gifts is how I am of service to illuminate a customized path to unlocking and releasing blocks, fears, and anger to bring people back to self-love so that they can soar higher in both their business and personal life."
~ Lisa Lamont

Lisa Lamont, The Modern Day Fortune Teller, is a renowned hypnotherapist, radio talk show host, and author. She created a powerful tool called "Mirror Love" that her clients incorporate into their lives to empower themselves in their quest for self-love. Long ago, Lisa was hand-picked by a famous psychic to inherit her powerful, one-of-a-kind Gypsy Cards and her teachings. Lisa has been reading these cards ever since--for over 30 years now.

Today, she combines the reading of the Gypsy Cards with her customized hypnotherapy techniques to help her clients gain greater insight and conquer problems that are holding them back in both their personal and business lives. She is truly passionate about sharing her intuitive gifts and helping her clients get amazing results.

Lisa also has created a safe and dynamic group for women called the Prancing Kittens, which got its name because just like cats, women always land on their feet! Her goal is to help women share their stories, inspirations, and unique points of view in an environment that is always encouraging, non-judgmental, and, most importantly, safe. Lisa is always looking for ways to empower women both in her community and around the world. She has a weekly radio blog show called Get Your Prance On that covers important topics and gives women a place to share their Voice. She is a genuine leader with a big heart.

MODERN DAY FORTUNE TELLER

I invite you to reach out and get to know Lisa Lamont and her company brand. She is truly a blessing, and I am grateful that she has joined the No.113 Branding Women Community. Cheers to you, Lisa!

Lisa Lamont   (206) 834-LISA
lisalamont@yahoo.com   www.LisaLamont.com

~EXERCISE~
What three articles can you create today?

TAKE 3: "CLIENT CHECK-INS"

Increase your consistency in communications and experience by checking in with clients often.

It is important to emotionally connect with your past and current clients. Remembering their birthday and anniversary, and celebrating their accomplishments is a beautiful way of honoring them.

Once a client is part of your company brand network, it is important to keep them in the fold.

~EXERCISE~
SET-UP A CHECK-IN CALENDAR AND INCLUDE
YOUR PAST AND CURRENT CLIENTS.

TAKE 4: ON-CAMERA APPEARANCES

As your company brand Visibility and Influence grows in the marketplace so will your on-camera appearances. Knowing how to make your dynamic qualities shine on-camera is essential for being successful in your field. It is important for you to learn professional techniques for letting your light shine just as brightly as the stars in Hollywood.

Your upcoming on-camera appearance is a great opportunity to build a relationship with the community and get the buzz out about your company brand. To help you take center stage with your next on-camera project, here are ten tips for a successful on-camera appearance.

TIP #1. BE PREPARED

Being prepared for your interview will help you to project your natural confidence on-screen. If possible, ask for a list of questions beforehand so that you can practice your responses. By anticipating the types of questions you may receive, you can practice your answers in the mirror. This will help you to respond quickly to questions and establish yourself as an authority on the subject matter.

~EXERCISE~

CREATE A SIMPLE SCRIPT THAT YOU CAN REFER TO
WHEN ASKING THE INTERVIEWER TO PROVIDE A
LIST OF QUESTIONS BEFOREHAND.

TIP #2. MAKE EYE CONTACT

As with any conversation, eye contact is important for establishing a personal connection with your audience. When speaking directly to a viewer through media such as Skype, be sure to look directly at the camera. If you are having a recorded face-to-face interview, then focus on making eye contact with your interviewer.

~EXERCISE~
HAVE A FRIEND FILM YOU ON THEIR PHONE
WHILE YOU PRACTICE ESTABLISHING EYE CONTACT.

TIP #3. DO YOUR RESEARCH

Always find out as much as possible about the person conducting your interview. Be sure to watch a few episodes of previously aired shows and make notes on your interviewer's personal style. This will help you to respond appropriately and avoid being caught off-guard by strange quirks.

~EXERCISE~
TAKE NOTES ON THE INTERVIEWER'S PERSONAL STYLE.

TIP #4. DRESS APPROPRIATELY

You will want to take extra care with your appearance when you take center stage. Be sure to dress appropriately for the occasion and remember that your fashion can make a major statement about your personal brand.

~EXERCISE~
HAVE A FRIEND TAKE PICTURES OF YOU IN A VARIETY
OF DIFFERENT OUTFITS AND DISCUSS TOGETHER
WHICH ONE LOOKS BEST ON-CAMERA.

TIP #5. USE TELEVISION MAKEUP

On-camera, stage lights can create a shiny, washed-out face if you are not careful to apply the right type of makeup. Generally, on-camera makeup should be applied slightly heavier than normal to avoid shine and to bring out your best features.

~EXERCISE~
TAKE THE TIME TO APPLY YOUR MAKEUP BEFORE THE DAY OF YOUR BIG ON-CAMERA INTERVIEW AND TAKE PICTURES AND REVIEW THEM SO THAT YOU LOOK HOLLYWOOD READY.

TIP #6. WATCH YOUR BODY LANGUAGE

On-camera viewers tune in to more than just your words. Therefore, you will want to make sure your body language matches your message. Avoid using overly large gestures and fidgeting. By using calm and relaxed movements, you will captivate your audience with your self-confident style.

~EXERCISE~
REHEARSE IN FRONT OF THE MIRROR AND WATCH YOUR GESTURES CLOSELY. MAKE ADJUSTMENTS ACCORDINGLY AND APPLY WHAT YOU LEARNED.

TIP #7. REMEMBER TO SMILE

A smile always makes a person more attractive. Throughout your interview, make sure to smile so that you will seem friendly and approachable.

It may feel uncomfortable smiling throughout your interview, but it tells the audience that you are warm and approachable.

~EXERCISE~
PRACTICE SMILING FOR TEN MINUTES IN A ROW WITHOUT BREAKING YOUR SMILE.

Tip #8. Avoid Distractions

During an on-camera interview, you will want to eliminate any distractions that may appear. Leave your cell phone behind, never chew gum, and try to avoid sitting in a swivel-style chair.

~EXERCISE~
Make a checklist of distractions and take it with you to be sure that you eliminate them during your on-camera appearance.

Tip #9. Stay Calm

During any recording, there are a thousand things that can suddenly occur. Therefore, remember to stay calm if your feed suddenly stops rolling or the technicians switch to a live broadcast. Remain flexible, and you will be certain to shine no matter what happens.

~EXERCISE~
Incorporate a breathing exercise into your routine before going on-camera.

Tip #10. Always Rehearse

Rehearsing prior to your interview is the best way to alleviate stress so that you can deliver your message with the calm demeanor and confident style that you are known for. When rehearsing, be sure to use all of the previous techniques so that you can gain greater Visibility and Influence for you and your company brand and take center stage at your next on-camera interview.

~EXERCISE~
Have a friend record a rehearsal on your phone and review it together. Take detailed notes and make changes accordingly.

Superstar Spotlight Tips

1. Branding is an on-going juggling act of marketing, research, and conversation.

2. Provide VIP service, as it will increase your brand influence.

3. Your website will serve as nothing more than a business card if you are not sharing your expertise in your field. Give people a reason to come back to check out your brand.

4. If your business is having a hard time jumping to the next level of success it might be time for a brand refresh.

5. Write an eBook that shares expertise about your brand.

~EXERCISE~
FILL IN FIVE OF YOUR OWN TIPS THAT YOU CAN SHARE WITH THE MARKETPLACE.

Step out of the shadows and into the Spotlight.

113 BRANDING

ACT III:
TURN UP THE SPOTLIGHT ON YOUR VISIBILITY AND INFLUENCE WITH SOCIAL MEDIA

*G*ain greater Visibility and Influence by leveraging your social media business platforms. In today's marketplace, it is essential to strengthen ties to the community. You can use your social media business platforms to get input from your current customers and convert your most committed customers into "brand evangelists" who help spread your company brand message across the platforms.

Social media has radically changed the way entrepreneurs approach marketing. Before social media came along, entrepreneurs relied on one-way communication and "push" marketing tactics like print and direct mail.

Instead of the one-to-many marketing, entrepreneurs can now communicate with consumers on a person-to-person level. Unlike traditional marketing, social media has empowered the consumer. This empowerment has increased the importance of word-of-mouth marketing. Now, instead of telling one or two friends, you can tell hundreds or even thousands of your social media connections in just a matter of seconds.

WHAT MAKES SOCIAL MEDIA DIFFERENT FROM TRADITIONAL MARKETING?

1. It is interactive.

2. It is free.

3. You can get the message out about your brand instantly.

4. It is your own private marketing machine that can gain you and your brand Visibility and Influence quickly.

~EXERCISE~
KEEP YOUR SOCIAL MEDIA USERNAMES AND PASSWORDS IN ONE PLACE FOR EASY ACCESS BELOW.

TAKE 1: PROVIDE REAL VALUE

It is important when sharing your company brand message across your social media channels to provide "Real Value" for the marketplace by offering tools, techniques, and tips that people can easily incorporate.

This allows the marketplace to know, like and trust your company brand.

No one wants to be "sold to." Instead, the marketplace wants to get to know your company brand first.

Tip: Maintain a low overhead and manage your cash flow effectively so that your brand has a chance to thrive.

113 BRANDING

IDENTIFY EIGHT TANGIBLES THAT ADD REAL VALUE FOR
YOU AND YOUR COMPANY BRAND IN THE MARKETPLACE.

TAKE 2: Spotlight Other Brands

When you spotlight other brands across your company brand's social media channels, the spotlight will turn back to shine directly on your brand.

People support those who they know support them. It will organically increase your company brand Visibility and Influence.

Always lead from your heart and a place of integrity when choosing what company brands you will spotlight.

> *When you turn the spotlight on other brands, you will find the spotlight turning back to shine directly on your brand. People support those who they know support them. This 113 Branding strategy only works when you are leading from your heart and a place of integrity.*

~EXERCISE~

CREATE A LIST OF ALL THE PEOPLE THAT YOU CAN SPOTLIGHT AND INCLUDE ONE HIGHLIGHT THAT YOU CAN SHARE ABOUT THEIR BRAND ACROSS YOUR SOCIAL MEDIA CHANNELS. BE SURE TO TAG THE PERSON WHEN POSTING.

Double and Triple Dip Your Way to Massive Brand Visibility

The Double Dip is a brilliant simple strategy that moves brand visibility to a whole new level.

Based on community building and leverage, it is a delectable way to get noticed without hogging the limelight. This tactic allows two company brands to meld their ideas into a media partnership, and design a gourmet treat to highlight both parties! The Double Dip can gain you and your company brand delicious visibility in the marketplace.

Follow these 5 easy steps to a visible taste sensation.

How The Double Dip Works

1. Network with other like-minded company brand owners to find an organic mix and match. Whoever initiates the Double Dip conversation takes charge.

2. Keep it simple. Do something as low key as asking brand number 2 to supply a "quote" that ties into one of your upcoming posts. Even sweeter is when you collaborate on the idea. Select a mutually significant topic, each player supplying a slant that is all their own. You and your brand partner can choose from an array of social media options to produce a video, podcast, article, blog, or series of tweets that highlight your chosen topic. Be sure to spotlight the other brand's contributions positively in your media; the secret sauce is all in the teamwork.

3. It's the big day! Both you and your partner need to publish the cross-pollinated content simultaneously across all of your social media to ensure maximum exposure. Don't forget to tag each other to heighten the delicious taste sensation.

4. Be discerning. Always post your social media in groups that complement your message and company brand.

5. Don't stop with one Double Dip. Keep the sweetness flowing

by cross-pollinating in new and succulent ways. Look for brands that have a similar target market to help you launch that next interactive double.

WHAT IS THE BENEFIT OF DOUBLE DIPPING?

When you turn the spotlight on other brands, you will find the spotlight turning back to shine directly on your brand. First, you are leveraging each other's net worth, which can lead to greater sales not only for your brand, but also for those that you're associated with—which increases your marketability with other community brands.

Additionally, you promote positive communications between company brand owners—not just those in your area, but those nationally and worldwide. This makes for amazing opportunities for you to help each other attain what you've been looking for: Brand Visibility.

113 BRANDING

Think Triple Delicious!

The Double Dip is a delicious starting point, but you haven't heard it all.

The Triple Dip is a flavorful community-building strategy for business owners who are ready to take it to the next level.

How The Triple Dip Works

With the intention of scooping up each other's net worth and boosting community, three brands forge a plan to strategically coordinate their chosen social media creation together, thereby highlighting all of their brands. Released at the same time, it's a veritable supernova of brand visibility.

The Triple Dip strategy provides endless benefits. It promotes positive and widespread visibility for your brand. Additionally, your brand's exposure will not only bring about new opportunities, but it will also open up conversations with other brands, boosting a community-building opportunity.

Start today — comb your network, and see how The Double Dip and/or The Triple Dip could work for your brand and for the brands in your community. There is power in numbers. Heads Up! Any collaborative venture must always be based on mutual respect, reciprocated energy, complete authenticity, and trust. There are no limits to how you can up your Visibility and Influence game with the double and triple dip!

TAKE 3: Professional Content

Share your expertise through producing content across your company brand social media channels.

Articles, blog posts, eBooks, etc. provide real value for the marketplace as well as support you as an expert in your field.

This allows the marketplace to emotionally connect with your company brand.

~EXERCISE~

LIST ALL YOUR CURRENT PROFESSIONAL CONTENT AND
KEEP A RUNNING LIST SO THAT YOU CAN BE SHARING
IT WITH THE MARKETPLACE OFTEN.

~EXERCISE~
MAKE A LIST OF PROFESSIONAL CONTENT THAT YOU STILL NEED TO CREATE.

TAKE 4: BE CONSISTENT

TIP #1. MAKE TIME FOR SOCIAL MEDIA

Being consistent daily and uploading content to your social media platforms is a major key to increasing your company brand Visibility and Influence.

Saying things like, "I don't have time for social media" is like saying "I don't care about driving customers to my company brand or increasing my business bottom-line."

Creating a four-week calendar in advance is a great way to stay on track and not get overwhelmed with what you are going to share daily on social media.

~EXERCISE~
LAY OUT A FOUR-WEEK CALENDAR TO REFER TO DAILY BY INCLUDING THE DATE AND ITEM THAT YOU WILL BE SHARING.

Tip #2. Always Grow Your Online Net Worth

Make it a priority to grow your online numbers across all of your social media platforms. The larger your online net worth the stronger your Visibility and Influence for your company brand.

~EXERCISE~
Fill-in your current social media numbers and set an intention to double them by the end of the year.

Facebook #:

Facebook Biz #:

Twitter #:

LinkedIn #:

Instagram #:

Tip #3. Find Ways To Engage

Ask questions that people will be interested in. You want to talk about your interests, ideas, books, music, etc. It helps create brand trust. Like-minded people gravitate to like-minded people. Sharing your personal interests allows the marketplace to get to know you on a three-dimensional level, and that translates into increasing your Visibility and Influence for you and your company brand.

~EXERCISE~
LIST ALL OF YOUR INTERESTS BELOW:

Tip #4. Blog Weekly

Blogging is a great way of driving numbers to your social media platforms and increasing your Visibility and Influence. It is also a great way to leverage yourself as an expert in your field.

~EXERCISE~

Pick five topics that support your company brand that you can blog about.

Superstar Spotlight Tips

1. Never wear black or white when taking your branded headshots.

2. Have a good logo design created. It creates trust with consumers about your brand.

3. Facebook Pages are now an essential part of an online brand presence.

4. The minute you step outside the door you are an extension of your brand. Brand yourself so that people remember you and allow your unique personality to shine brightly.

5. Clean out your email box weekly. It will help keep your brand streamlined.

~EXERCISE~
FILL IN FIVE OF YOUR OWN TIPS THAT YOU CAN SHARE WITH THE MARKETPLACE.

Visibility
&
Influence
Are
Always
In Style
113 BRANDING

THE PREMIERE:
TURNING UP THE VISIBILITY AND INFLUENCE
SPOTLIGHT STARRING 113 BRANDING

*W*hen developing your customized social media marketing campaign for your company brand to gain more Visibility and Influence in the marketplace, you want to keep in mind that the key is to be interesting and not predictable.

You want the marketplace to stop and take notice. You want to send out a signal in the marketplace that is in alignment with you and your brand so that your Ideal Client is attracted to your brand.

For example: Let's suppose you are an entrepreneur in the sales field. The predictable approach would be to incorporate images of dollar signs and money. Money and sales can evoke emotions of anxiety and fear within people in the marketplace. Instead you want to incorporate imagery that tells a story, that grabs the attention of the marketplace, and that is interesting. Imagery that is warm and approachable and takes the emotional sting out of sales. Imagery that tells people that you truly care about making the process of their work with you a wonderful experience.

Keep in mind that branding is just an extension of who you are. You want to evoke an inner essence that is in alignment with who you are and what you want to convey to the marketplace.

Enclosed is a preview of the 113 Branding Social Media Visibility and Influence Marketing Campaign. My song is Visibility and Influence and I support my song with verses that emotionally connect with people in the marketplace. My campaign is designed to call in my Ideal Client.

I tell my brand story with vibrant images, typically of women, that describe my unique point-of-view on the importance for entrepreneurs to step out of the shadows and step into their Spotlight. To grow their company brand Visibility and Influence because it is directly linked to their brand's earning power.

Branding is like denim. It fits and feels better the more you wear it.
113 BRANDING

113 Branding Online
Marketing Image Campaign

Each image is customized with original 113 Branding key branding and uploaded across all the social media channels to increase visibility and brand influence.

113 Online Marketing Virtual Magazine

Virtual magazines are a great way to spotlight your company brand as well as shining the spotlight on clients. You can also share content like blogs, videos, articles, images, and more. It is a sexy way to gain greater visibility and brand influence.

For example: 113 Branding VIP Issue

MEET SHERILL CALHOUN

FEMPRENEUR NETWORK
Leading main street fempreneurs to the finish line!

During the month of March, I attended a great networking event in the heart of San Francisco that was sponsored by Square. Square's main floor has a size advantage that many offices don't; it spans the length of an entire city block, with about 100,000 square feet of space, enough to cover two football fields…very impressive, indeed. The name of the event was "Ladies Who Launch – Celebrating Women Entrepreneurs".

I must admit, it was another "first" for me in several ways, although certainly not my first networking event. I attended at the invitation of another Super Connector friend and business associate of mine, Joie Gharrity, Founder of No.113 Branding. We both went to the event to catch up on business and enjoy the evening, but also to implement a strategy to leverage our brands and philosophy relative to fempreneurs.

Both the staff and guests attending the event were very warm…well except for the young woman that I sat down and introduced myself to just before Sarah Friar, CFO of Square, welcomed us all. I turned to her with a smile and extended my hand to initiate a connection. She had been intensely texting before my introduction as if to use her phone as a shield for ignoring everyone around her. She seemed very uncomfortable with my outreach and when I turned my head to ask what her line of business was, she had moved to another location in the room. That was a "first" for me. Some might have felt offended by that gesture, others may have never even noticed, but I understood the painful awkwardness that can accompany the networking process, especially for those who are new to the practice.

Yet other exciting firsts that evening were:

- My first time at Square Headquarters in San Francisco.

- The first time I ever met Jack Dorsey, CEO of Square and Co-Founder of Twitter.

- The first time I ever met Maria Contreras-Sweet, U. S. SBA administrator for the Obama Cabinet.

- The first time I ever met Julia Hart, Co-founder and President of Eventbrite.

www.thefempreneurnetwork.net

113Branding.com   -3-

FOR EXAMPLE: 113 BRANDING SPOTLIGHT
STARRING CAT WILLIFORD,
INNER GAME COACH FOR WOMEN, SPEAKER, AND AUTHOR

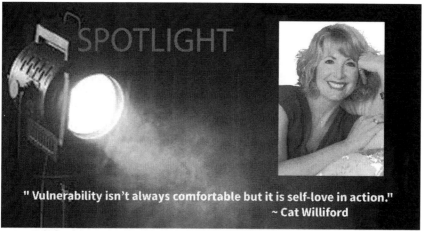

" Vulnerability isn't always comfortable but it is self-love in action."
~ Cat Williford

Cat Williford is a Transformational Self-Development Coach, International Speaker, Author, Wise Woman, and Conversation Starter. She is a recognized pioneer in the Coaching professional.

For 20+ years she has helped thousands of high achieving, pioneering, creative thinking, message-driven women leaders achieve lasting results and success. Of course, she believes every outer world success stems from what she calls Inner Game Strategies. She has experienced and witnessed friends and clients struggle with similar issues: perfectionism, control, fear and pretending to be who someone else wants them to be.

Cat's background in theatre, mythology and esoteric wisdom informed her Inner Game Strategy system. Her system guides women to remove their modern day archetypal masks and start living what she calls The Authenticity Advantage. Her clients discover newfound levels of self-love, confidence, freedom, choice, vulnerability and strength.

She also spreads her message of self-love and authenticity as an international speaker, writer, and frequent guest expert on TV, radio and print. She openly shares her story of overcoming a car-train wreck and a debilitating sense of failure when her father died shortly after she donated a kidney to him, so that others will know that there is no challenge that we cannot overcome.

I invite you to get to know Cat Williford. She is a blessing, and I am grateful that she has joined the No.113 Branding Women community. Cheers to you Cat!

Vision Steps   (805) 271-1155
Cat Williford - CEO   Cat@CatWilliford.com
www.catwilliford.com

113 ONLINE MARKETING VIDEO TRAILERS

Video trailers are a great way to spotlight your brand and tell your brand story. It is a way to entertain the marketplace and gain greater visibility and brand influence.

FOR EXAMPLE: 113 BRANDING VIDEO SPOTLIGHT
STARRING SHEILA KENNEDY,
CEO/FOUNDER THE ZEBRA INC. PUBLISHING

"Choices To Changes"
https://vimeo.com/149369017

FOR EXAMPLE: 113 BRANDING VIDEO SPOTLIGHT STARRING LUCY GRECO, REAL ESTATE PROFESSIONAL CAL BRE #01880917

"Where You Live Shapes Your Life"
https://vimeo.com/153982541

"Where you live shapes your life."
Lucy Greco

Hollywood Diaries:

My Blockbuster Moments

INFLUENCE HANDED ME THE
HOLLYWOOD GOLDEN TICKET

In my early 20's, I ran with a fabulous group of girlfriends in San Francisco. We were all about glamour. We draped ourselves in pearls, wore Coco Chanel perfume, and never left the house without our red lipstick. We spent all of our dispensable income on elaborate dinner parties, buying glamorous party dresses, and getting our hair and makeup professionally done for a fabulous night out on the town. We shared our hopes and dreams with one another over cocktails.

One of our favorite topics was travel. We would talk for hours about all the places like Egypt, France, and Italy that we hoped to visit as if we had already been there. We would weave stories about all the adventures we had and all the fascinating people we had met. On my birthday that year my friends showered me with Egyptian trinkets, and books about The Nile. I was thrilled with my new treasures.

We decided that we would travel as a group, and our first destination would be Egypt. We started saving our money, researching ticket prices, accommodations, and more. We set the date and were beyond excited about our upcoming journey.

My priorities started shifting. I still enjoyed the glamorous lifestyle, but I was eager to embark on a professional career.

A good friend of mine with influence offered me an opportunity to meet his brother who was a famous agent in Los Angeles. This friend of mine offered to ask his brother to use his influence to secure a job for me in the Hollywood entertainment industry. He told me that if I was packed and moved a week from that day he would meet me at Bob's Big Boy in Burbank and make the introduction. I immediately said yes.

I informed my family that I was moving to Hollywood, and they were not enthusiastic about my decision. They felt that it was a reckless decision and asked me to reconsider. I was determined in my decision and went anyway. I met my friend's brother, and he was able to get me an interview with an up-and-coming SCI-FI Director and his Production team. I got the job working as an Assistant to the Producer. It was a very exciting time in my life.

A few weeks after being hired, we all traveled from Los Angeles to the desert dunes of Yuma, Arizona, and went into production. Arriving on the *Stargate* set, I was shocked and astonished to be standing in front of a seven-story high Egyptian Pyramid sitting in the middle of the desert dunes.

The power of dreaming big and the assistance of two influencers who believed in me and my abilities transcended my dream of taking a trip to Egypt and instead delivered me a career in the movie business. It wasn't until recently, that I bridged the events leading up to *Stargate* and the power of influence.

Since returning to the Bay Area I opened my own business 113 Branding, and I share branding and marketing strategies with entrepreneurs globally. I have grown my own influence in the marketplace so that I can share it with others. I have built a virtual studio that gains my clients Visibility and Influence so that they can become their own superstars, stand in their spotlight and shine bright.

My dreams and intentions have changed since my early 20's, yet my love for the element of surprise has not. I am always eager to see how new Pyramids are going to show up in my life, and I am always grateful when they do.

How Working In Hollywood Taught Me The Power Of YES

Early in my career I was a script development girl. In other words, I would read endless scripts daily looking for great material for my boss, a Hollywood Movie Producer.

He offered me an opportunity to attend the Cannes Film Festival held in Cannes, France, with him so we could look for upcoming talent and potential projects. The Cannes Film Festival is the largest and most glamorous festival in the world. This was a big opportunity, and I said yes.

When we arrived in Cannes, he informed me that I would be on my own during the day and I was to attend the buyer and sales film convention to look for potential projects and make connections. We would only meet at night for dinner, and I would be expected to download him on the potential projects and connections that I made.

I summoned up my courage and I attended the buyer and sales film convention alone. Thankfully, the company I worked for had a growing "buzz" in Europe so as soon as I started introducing myself around the convention center, buyers and sellers started offering me invitations to attend fabulous parties and movie screenings.

One well-known buyer offered me an opportunity to accompany him to film screenings that only VIPs were allowed to attend. This was a big opportunity and I said yes. He picked me up at my hotel on a red Vespa. I jumped on the back and off we went zipping through the streets of Cannes.

He introduced me to a young movie producer from Los Angeles, and we became fast friends. This young producer invited me to come and meet him in the morning at his hotel for breakfast. I invited my boss to attend, but he informed me that this opportunity was too small so he said no.

The following morning, I handed the cab driver the address, and $60.00 later I arrived at the Hotel du Cap. The Hotel du Cap is one of the most famous hotels in the world, located on the French Riviera. When I saw my boss that evening for dinner, he was floored by my experience.

After returning to Los Angeles, this young movie producer invited me to his incredible home in Santa Monica for a dinner party. It turns out that he was an Influencer. The next day when I arrived at the office and told my boss about this grand dinner party and all the influential people that I was introduced to, he regretted his decision of saying no in Cannes.

As an entrepreneur, you might always be looking for that big break or big opportunity for you and your brand. But I encourage you to say yes even if you think the opportunity might look small. Big things can come out of it.

LISTENING TO YOUR GUT CAN LEAD TO UNEXPECTED GEMS

Early in my career as a Script Girl, I had a script come across my desk that at first I was not interested in reading because the synopsis read: *Ben Sanderson, an alcoholic Hollywood screenwriter who lost everything because of his drinking, arrives in Las Vegas to drink himself to death. There, he meets and forms an uneasy friendship and non-interference pact with prostitute Sera.* My "gut" told me to read the script anyway, and I did reluctantly.

It turned out that I fell in love with the script and genuinely felt compassion for the characters. I knew this was a "gem" and this project was going to do well. I encouraged my boss to pursue the project, but, unfortunately, we were not able to secure it. The project *Leaving Las Vegas* went on to star Nicolas Cage and Elisabeth Shue and was a big hit. Moving forward, I realized the importance of keeping an open mind and following my gut. It would lead to doors of golden opportunity.

As an entrepreneur, being open to following your "gut" and not judging a "book by its cover" is important. There are going to be doors of opportunities that will cross your desk and at first glance might not look like much.

I encourage my clients to start really trusting and following their "gut" because it can lead to so many unexpected "gems."

FIERCELY PROTECT YOUR BRAND

When I worked in the Hollywood entertainment industry, I had the pleasure of getting to work on the Sony studio lot. In the middle of the lot was a cobblestone Main Street lined with storefronts like a soda fountain, ice cream parlor, and a women's hat department. It looked as if it was pulled directly out of the iconic movie *Singing In The Rain* with Gene Kelly.

When family and friends would come to visit, at first glance they thought the storefronts were real—but in reality it was just a façade.

Early in my career, I learned that if something seemed too good to be true then it was. Being able to see past the façade and see what is really behind the red curtains was essential in both my personal and professional life. I would meet people along the way who would claim that they could make the right introductions and get me a seat at the right dinner tables. In reality, they were just dreamers and there were no real tangibles behind their red curtains.

As an entrepreneur, you might run across people who claim the same. They claim they can make the right introductions and get you a seat at the right dinner tables so you can make bigger dollars and cents. Perhaps they even charge you big dollars in the form of "packages" to make that happen. In reality, it takes years to build deep connections and just because someone sits you at a table with high-level entrepreneurs doesn't guarantee they are going to want to take the relationship to the next level.

Real business relationships are built from the ground up based on trust and emotional connections. I encourage my clients to pull back the red curtains so they don't waste money and time. I encourage them to fiercely protect their brand.

The only person who can protect your brand is you, and your brand is a precious resource so please take care of it.

Grow Your Tribe and Your Brand Will Soar

When I landed my first job in Hollywood on the movie set, I knew that it was essential that I surround myself with my "tribe." So I asked the 1st Assistant Director about my brother and my friend who would make great production assistants on the set.

He was very gracious and said yes. I informed my brother and my friend that it was a green light and they had only a few days to arrive in town if they were to secure their positions.

Fast forward to us being on the movie set in the scorching heat of the Yuma desert and working very long hours. It was an exciting experience, and it made it more exciting to get to share it with my "tribe" members. All three of us continued to work in the Hollywood entertainment business and continued to grow our tribe over the years.

When I first launched my business, 113 Branding, it was an exciting time but very isolating. I hadn't built up a "tribe" in the Bay Area yet. I learned very quickly how important it is to surround yourself with a community of like-minded people. Even though my business is a solo business, having a "tribe" makes for a more exciting experience and having a support system is essential.

As an entrepreneur in order to authentically grow your "tribe" network that is going to have your back, there needs to be an equal exchange of energy, trust, and respect. The house of cards will fall if your attitude is always "What can you do for me?" or "I did this for you so now what are you going to do for me?" Instead, your attitude should be "What can we do for each other?" "How can we both be of service to one another and our brands?"

I encourage you to reach out to your tribe often and ask how you all can be "of" service to one another. There is power in numbers. As long as the "tribe" is authentically showing up for each other and there is an equal exchange of energy, trust, and respect, you can move mountains and all of your brands will soar.

It's a Wrap

*A*s an entrepreneur, I am passionate about being of service and supporting entrepreneurs globally. I am proud of the personal and professional brand that I have developed. I enjoy that I am no longer dependent on another brand for my Visibility or Influence—that has given me a great sense of freedom.

I have found that with freedom comes great responsibility. There are days I don't feel like being visible or growing my influence in the marketplace, but I push myself to stand in my spotlight anyway. I have learned the valuable lessons that the brand level of Visibility and Influence in the marketplace directly impacts a constant stream of customers and a thriving business.

I encourage you all to be of service and develop your own personal and professional brand so that you do not find yourself dependent. When you are dependent on another brand, the possibility that one day that brand might no longer be viable—or even worse may no longer enlist your services—could become a reality.

As an entrepreneur, the greater your influence, the bigger the business opportunities that will be presented to you and the more likely that your brand will thrive and soar higher and higher. Even if you are currently working for a corporation, growing your personal and professional brand can be an asset. The more influence you bring into the room, the greater leverage you will have for job security, longevity, and promotions.

Entrepreneurs always ask me how long it takes to gain Visibility and Influence that will make a real impact on their brand and increase their business revenue. If you are consistent, authentic, and incorporate the enclosed strategies, techniques, and tips, while working on your inner game, it can happen very quickly. Within a year and a half, my brand has tripled in business and the opportunities that have come my way because of my Visibility and Influence have been game changers.

Recently, I traveled back to Hollywood for business and ended up staying for five months. I never thought I would go back to Los Angeles, but I am so glad I did. It was an incredible experience. It gave me the opportunity to revisit my old haunting grounds, face old stories, and reconnect with old friends. It served as another reminder that life is a beautiful journey.

Growing your Visibility and Influence can be emotional at times. Stepping into your spotlight takes courage. You will have to dig deep and find your second wind.

Always keep in mind that it is a gift for you to share your brand, talents, and gifts with the community and the world. You are deserving of making your dreams come true and of living an abundant and prosperous life.

My hope is to connect with you, whether it is online or in person. I believe in you, and I am cheering you on.

Remind yourself daily that it is your birthright to shine bright, sweet friend.

You are loved and appreciated!

Cheers,

Joie Gharrity

My sincere gratitude
to the following ...

Dennis Gharrity - Your willingness to jump off cliffs and go after your dreams made a huge impact on me growing up. I wouldn't be who I am today without your constant support and encouragement!

Sheila Kennedy - Thank you for saying yes to publishing my book and supporting my creative spirit. I will always be grateful to you, Sister!

Heather Leineweber Robison - Thank you for sharing your creative gifts and talents with the world and me. You are a blessing, sweet friend!

Lisa Lamont - Your talents and gifts have been a true game changer both in my personal and professional life. Thank you, Soul Sister!

Roland Emmerich - Your mentorship and friendship helped shape the person I am today. Thank you!

Michelle Radomski - Your talent is a major blessing. Thank you for saying yes to being on the team, Sister!

Madlen Saddik - Your unwavering support is appreciated big time, Sister. You make my heart sing!

Mark Pedowitz - Thank you for believing in me. Your ongoing support means the world to me!

Jen Duchene - Soul Sister, thank you for all your support and encouragement. Your gifts and talents have been a game changer!

Sherill Calhoun – Sister, thank you for supporting me on this crazy cool journey. Keep being a warrior, sweet friend.

Angela Mosley - Thank you for sharing your gift and talents. You made the editing process a beautiful one. I am grateful for all your support.

Stacy Bloodworth - You are beautiful both inside and out. Your talent for taking an incredible picture is truly a blessing.

Corina Ciont - Your continued support has been a huge gift Sister. Thank you for sharing your expertise about money and value with me.

ABOUT THE AUTHOR

*J*oie Gharrity, founder of 113 Branding, is a Brand Strategist, Marketer, Content Developer, and Speaker. She worked in the Hollywood entertainment industry for 15+ years at top companies, such as Centropolis Entertainment, The Walt Disney Company, and Sony Pictures, in film, television, original web content, and branded entertainment. She was encouraged and taught branding, marketing, and networking techniques by high-level mentors.

After returning to the Bay Area, Joie was inspired to launch 113 Branding. She integrates her strategic branding and marketing vision coupling the creative and business aspects of the entertainment industry. Her techniques and strategies help entrepreneurs globally become more Visible, Influential, and Successful.

To connect with Joie, please visit www.113branding.com.

Made in the USA
Middletown, DE
17 June 2017